I0867287

SCIENCE ESSENTIALS
FORCE AND MOTION
This book belongs to
Wonder House

FORCE

IT CAN MAKE THINGS MOVE
EITHER BY A PUSH OR PULL

TO MAKE A CAR RACE
OR LET IT JUST REMAIN IN PLACE

THINGS CAN CHANGE THEIR SHAPE
OR CAN EVEN ESCAPE

ALL THIS HAS ONE SOURCE
IT'S NONE OTHER THAN FORCE!

WHAT IS FORCE ?
A FORCE IS A PUSH OR PULL ON AN OBJECT.
PUSH
A PUSH IS A FORCE EXERTED AWAY FROM THE BODY. FOR EXAMPLE, PUSHING A LAWN MOWER, KICKING A FOOTBALL.
THE GIRL PUSHES THE LAWN MOWER **AWAY** FROM HER.
THE GIRL IS PULLING THE DOG'S LEASH **TOWARDS** HER.
FORCES ALWAYS HAVE A DIRECTION IN WHICH THEY ACT.
PULL
PULL
A PULL IS A FORCE EXERTED TOWARDS THE BODY. FOR EXAMPLE, PULLING A DOG'S LEASH, PLAYING TUG OF WAR.
PULL
PULL

WHAT CAN FORCE DO?
IT CAN MAKE AN OBJECT:
MOVE
SPEED UP
SLOW DOWN
CHANGE DIRECTION
CHANGE SHAPE
LET'S PLAY
TURN

TYPES OF FORCES

CONTACT FORCES

FORCES THAT REQUIRE A TOUCH OR CONTACT TO BE APPLIED ARE KNOWN AS CONTACT FORCES. FOR EXAMPLE, MUSCULAR FORCE AND FRICTIONAL FORCE.

NON-CONTACT FORCES

FORCES THAT DO NOT NEED A CONTACT OR THAT HAVE THEIR INFLUENCE WITHOUT A TOUCH ARE NON-CONTACT FORCES. FOR EXAMPLE: MAGNETIC FORCE, ELECTROSTATIC FORCE, GRAVITATIONAL FORCE.

CONTACT FORCES

THERE ARE DIFFERENT TYPES OF CONTACT FORCES. EACH FORCE REFERS TO A SPECIFIC CONDITION.

SLEEPING ON A RUG
CONTAINERS OF FOOD ON A KITCHEN SHELF
NORMAL FORCE
THE FORCE HERE IS APPLIED BETWEEN THE BOOK AND THE TABLE , I.E., TWO OBJECTS
SITTING ON THE GROUND
LEANING ON A WALL
GLASS OF WATER ON A TABLE

CLIMBING A MOUNTAIN USING A ROPE
CHEST FLY MACHINE
SUSPENSION BRIDGE
TENSION FORCE
IT'S THE PULLING FORCE. IT OCCURS IN ROPES, STRINGS OR WIRES WHEN THEY ARE PULLED TIGHTLY FROM BOTH ENDS.
CABLE IN AN ELEVATOR THAT LIFTS AND LOWERS IT
CRANE LIFTING OBJECTS
A CAR BEING TOWED BY ANOTHER VEHICLE

BUTTONS ON A KEYBOARD
BUNGEE CORDS
SPRING TOYS OR WATCHES
SPRING FORCE
A FORCE THAT ACTS WHEN A SPRING IS STRETCHED OR COMPRESSED BY AN OBJECT THAT IS ATTACHED TO IT.
A TRAMPOLINE
WATER SPRINKLERS IN A LAWN

FLYING AIRPLANE
PAPER PLANES
SKYDIVING
THE CYCLIST CROUCHES DOWN TO REDUCE THE AIR RESISTANCE.
STREAMLINED HELMETS ALSO HELP IN REDUCING AIR RESISTANCE.
AIR RESISTANCE
THE FORCE EXERTED ON AN OBJECT WHEN IT COMES IN CONTACT WITH AIR BY TRAVELING THROUGH IT. IT IS CAUSED BY FRICTION BETWEEN THE AIR AND THE OBJECT.
IN SUCH CASES, AIR RESISTANCE OPPOSES THE MOVEMENT OF THE OBJECT.
FLYING DOWN WITH A PARACHUTE
AN UMBRELLA FLYING AWAY ON A WINDY DAY

WRITING ON A PAPER WITH PENCIL
RUBBING HANDS
FRICTION WORKS AGAINST MOTION. HENCE, IT SLOWS DOWN A MOVING OBJECT. IT CAN ALSO HELP US TO CONTROL THE MOVEMENT OF OBJECTS.
APPLYING BRAKES
FRICTION
FRICTION IS A FORCE THAT IS CREATED WHEN TWO SURFACES RUB AGAINST EACH OTHER.
SLIDING DOWN THE SLIDES IN A PARK
FRICTION MAKES SURFACES STICK SLIGHTLY TOGETHER. IF THERE WAS NO FRICTION, WE WOULD SLIP AND SLIDE AROUND WHEN WE WALKED.
FOOTBALL PLAYERS WEAR CLEATS TO CREATE MORE FRICTION.

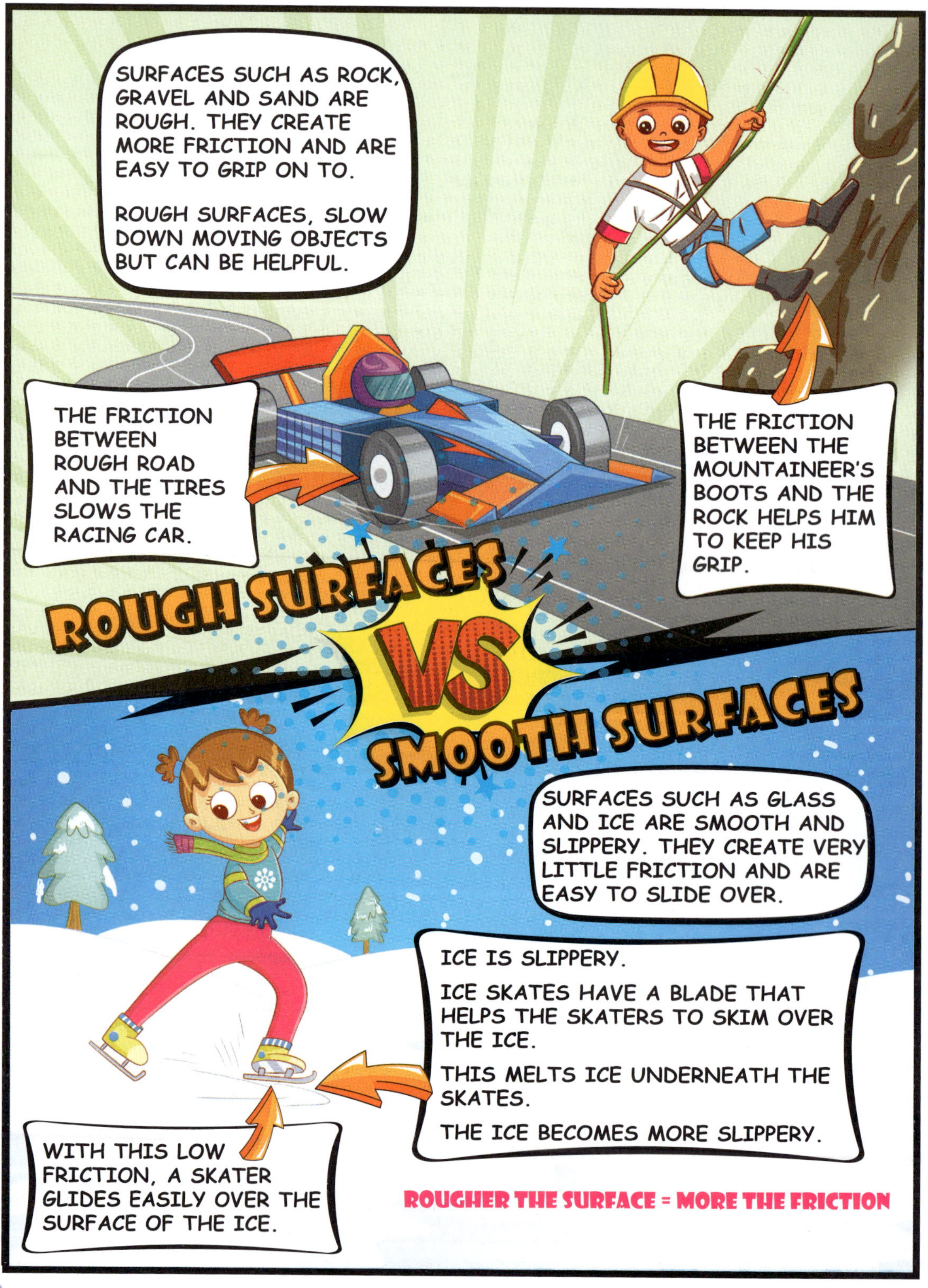
SURFACES SUCH AS ROCK, GRAVEL AND SAND ARE ROUGH. THEY CREATE MORE FRICTION AND ARE EASY TO GRIP ON TO.
ROUGH SURFACES, SLOW DOWN MOVING OBJECTS BUT CAN BE HELPFUL.
THE FRICTION BETWEEN ROUGH ROAD AND THE TIRES SLOWS THE RACING CAR.
THE FRICTION BETWEEN THE MOUNTAINEER'S BOOTS AND THE ROCK HELPS HIM TO KEEP HIS GRIP.
ROUGH SURFACES
VS
SMOOTH SURFACES
SURFACES SUCH AS GLASS AND ICE ARE SMOOTH AND SLIPPERY. THEY CREATE VERY LITTLE FRICTION AND ARE EASY TO SLIDE OVER.
ICE IS SLIPPERY.
ICE SKATES HAVE A BLADE THAT HELPS THE SKATERS TO SKIM OVER THE ICE.
THIS MELTS ICE UNDERNEATH THE SKATES.
THE ICE BECOMES MORE SLIPPERY.
WITH THIS LOW FRICTION, A SKATER GLIDES EASILY OVER THE SURFACE OF THE ICE.
ROUGHER THE SURFACE = MORE THE FRICTION

FRICTION
A NECESSARY EVIL
WITHOUT FRICTION, MANY ESSENTIAL TASKS SUCH AS WALKING, WRITING, LIFTING THINGS, STRIKING A FIRE, APPLYING BRAKES, ETC., CANNOT BE DONE.
LIFTING THINGS
WALKING
STRIKING A FIRE
APPLYING BRAKES
WRITING
DEAR SANTA
ON THE OTHER HAND, FRICTION ALSO RESULTS IN WEAR AND TEAR OF MACHINE PARTS AND LOSS OF ENERGY.
MACHINE PARTS WEAR OUT DUE TO FRICTION.
WHEN THE BLENDER RUNS FOR A FEW MINUTES, IT PRODUCES HEAT DUE TO FRICTION.
1 2 3 4 5 6 7 8 9 10 11 12 13 14 15 16
SO, WE CAN SAY THAT FRICTION IS A NECESSARY EVIL.

NON-CONTACT FORCES

NON-CONTACT FORCES OCCUR BETWEEN INTERACTIVE OBJECTS THAT ARE NOT IN PHYSICAL CONTACT WITH EACH OTHER; YET THEY EXERT PUSH OR PULL. ELECTRICAL FORCE, GRAVITATIONAL FORCE AND MAGNETIC FORCE ARE EXAMPLES OF NON-CONTACT FORCES.

ELECTRICAL FORCE

A FORCE THAT EXISTS BETWEEN ALL CHARGED PARTICLES.

PARTICLES CHARGED WITH ELECTRIC FORCES EITHER ATTRACT (PULL) OR REPEL (PUSH) EACH OTHER.

ALL OBJECTS ARE MADE OF ATOMS, WHICH CONTAIN A POSITIVELY CHARGED NUCLEUS AND NEGATIVELY CHARGED ELECTRONS. WHEN NEGATIVELY CHARGED ELECTRONS FLOW FROM ONE PLACE TO ANOTHER, ELECTRIC FORCE IS PRODUCED.

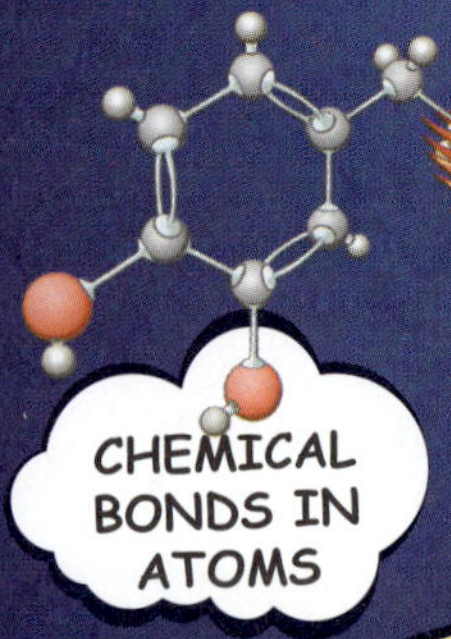

ELECTRIC EELS HAVE SPECIAL CELLS IN THEIR BODY THAT PRODUCE STRONG ELECTRIC DISCHARGES. THEY USE IT TO ELECTROCUTE OTHER FISH AND HUMANS TOO!

GRAVITATIONAL FORCE
A FORCE THAT ATTRACTS OBJECTS TOWARDS ONE ANOTHER. THE EARTH'S GRAVITATIONAL FORCE PULLS EVERYTHING TOWARDS IT.
ALL OBJECTS IN THE UNIVERSE HAVE THEIR OWN GRAVITY. THE HEAVIER ONES HAVE STRONGER GRAVITATIONAL FORCE THAN THE LIGHTER ONES.
PLANETS ARE HELD IN AN ORBIT IN THE SOLAR SYSTEM
THE DRINK IN A GLASS RESTS AT ITS BOTTOM
WE CAN WALK ON THE GROUND
DUE TO GRAVITY
WITHOUT GRAVITY WE WOULD FLOAT AWAY INTO THE SPACE
TIDES ARE CAUSED BY THE MOON'S GRAVITATIONAL PULL
A CAR COASTS DOWNHILL

MAGNETIC FORCE

A FORCE OF ATTRACTION OR REPULSION EXERTED BY A MAGNET.

MAGNETS ATTRACT OBJECTS MADE OF IRON, NICKEL AND COBALT TOWARDS THEM. THIS FORCE IS CALLED MAGNETISM.

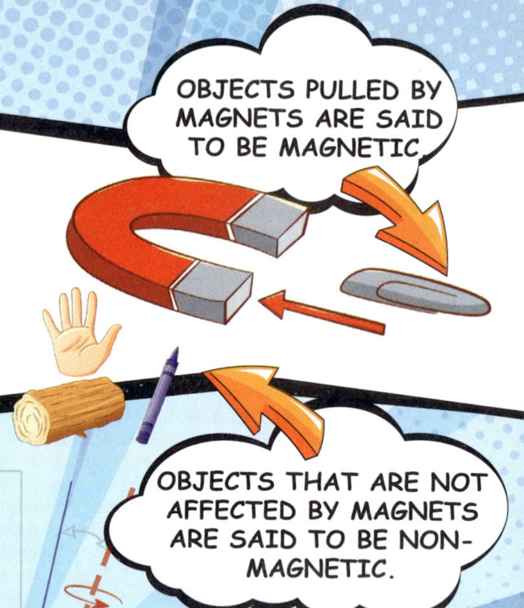

MAGNETIC FORCE IS OBSERVED IN

BALANCED AND UNBALANCED FORCES

FORCES CAN BE BALANCED OR UNBALANCED!

WHEN FORCES ON AN OBJECT ARE EQUAL AND ACT IN OPPOSITE DIRECTIONS, THEY ARE SAID TO BE BALANCED FORCES.

BALANCED FORCES DO NOT CAUSE ANY MOVEMENT.

TEAM - A IN THIS TUG OF WAR: **TEAM - B**

TEAM A, IS PULLING REALLY HARD, WITH ALL ITS STRENGTH!

TEAM B, IS ALSO PULLING WITH EQUAL STRENGTH AND FORCE!

THE FORCES OF TEAM A AND TEAM B ARE BALANCED ON THE ROPE. HENCE, IT DOES NOT MOVE!

WHEN THE FORCE APPLIED IN ONE DIRECTION IS GREATER THAN THE FORCE APPLIED IN THE OTHER (I.E. OPPOSITE) DIRECTION, IT RESULTS IN UNBALANCED FORCES.

UNBALANCED FORCES MAKE THINGS MOVE.

TEAM - C **TEAM - D**

HERE, TEAM C IS APPLYING MORE FORCE THAN TEAM D!

THE FORCE IS UNBALANCED HERE.

THERE IS MOVEMENT. TEAM C WINS!

MOTION

WHEN WE MOVE FROM HERE TO THERE
OR A BALLOON THAT FLIES INTO AIR.

TO DANCE AND SKATE, TO WALK AND FLY
OR MOVEMENT OF THE BIRDS IN THE SKY

REVOLUTION OF THE EARTH AROUND THE SUN
OR RISING TIDES IN THE OCEAN

WE ALSO CALL IT LOCOMOTION
IT'S NONE OTHER THAN MOTION!

WHAT IS MOTION?

MOTION IS THE PROCESS IN WHICH AN OBJECT OR PERSON MOVES OR CHANGES POSITION OR PLACE. FOR EXAMPLE, A BOY RUNNING, REVOLUTION OF EARTH AROUND THE SUN, MOVING OF FERRIS WHEEL IN A PARK.

WE CAN DESCRIBE THE MOTION OF AN OBJECT OR PERSON BY ITS SPEED. THE SPEED OF AN OBJECT SHOWS HOW FAST AN OBJECT IS MOVING OR MOVES.

$$\text{SPEED} = \frac{\text{DISTANCE TRAVELED BY A BODY}}{\text{THE TIME IT TAKES TO TRAVEL THAT DISTANCE}}$$

THE TIME WE TAKE TO TRAVEL A DISTANCE DEPENDS ON OUR SPEED. OBJECTS OR PEOPLE MOVING FAST COVER MORE DISTANCE IN A SHORTER TIME.

FIGHTER JET
1300 mph (2100km/h)

SPORTS CAR
180 mph (290km/h)

CHEETAH RUNNING
75 mph (120km/h)

RABBIT RUNNING
35 mph (56km/h)

HUMAN RUNNING
15 mph (25km/h)

TORTOISE WALKING
0.2 mph (0.3km/h)

A FIGHTER JET MOVES AT AN INCREDIBLE SPEED. THEY ARE DESIGNED IN SPECIFIC SHAPES, THAT WILL HELP THEM GLIDE THROUGH AIR SWIFTLY.

TYPES OF MOTION

LINEAR MOTION

THE MOVEMENT OF A BODY IN A STRAIGHT OR CURVED LINE WITHOUT ANY DEVIATION IS CALLED LINEAR MOTION. FOR EXAMPLE, A STONE FALLING FROM A HEIGHT, AN ATHLETE RUNNING ON A TRACK, ETC.

CIRCULAR MOTION

WHEN AN OBJECT CONSTANTLY MOVES IN A CIRCULAR PATH, IT IS SAID TO BE IN A CIRCULAR MOTION. FOR EXAMPLE, THE MOON REVOLVING AROUND THE EARTH, A BICYCLE MOVING ON A CIRCULAR TRACK, ETC.

PERIODIC MOTION

THE MOVEMENT OF AN OBJECT THAT IS REPEATED IN EQUAL INTERVALS OF TIME IS CALLED PERIODIC MOTION. FOR EXAMPLE, OSCILLATION OF A PENDULUM, A VIBRATING TUNING FORK, A ROCKING CHAIR, ETC.

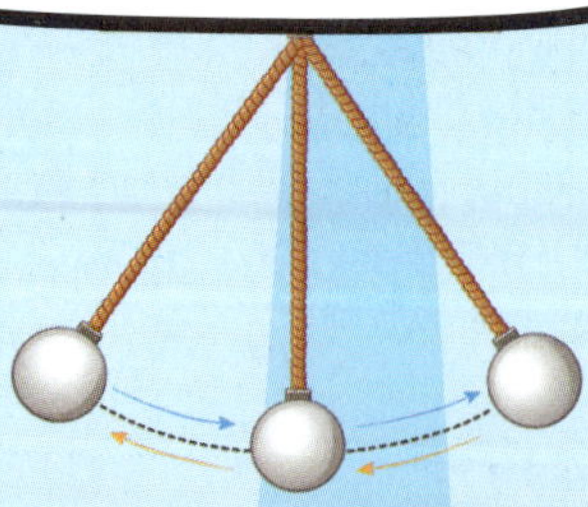

ROTATIONAL MOTION

WHEN A BODY MOVES OR SPINS ABOUT A FIXED AXIS, IT IS SAID TO BE IN ROTATIONAL MOTION. FOR EXAMPLE, A SPINNING TOP, THE TURNING OF BLADES OF A FAN, SPINNING OF EARTH ON ITS AXIS.

LAWS OF MOTION

THINGS CANNOT MOVE OR COME TO A HALT UNLESS ACTED UPON BY A FORCE. FORCES ALLOW US TO DO A NUMBER OF TASKS. THEY ALSO MOVE VEHICLES ALONG ROADS.

IN THE ABSENCE OF FORCES, NOTHING WOULD MOVE AND THE WORLD WOULD BE A STILL PLACE.

SIR ISAAC NEWTON CAME UP WITH THREE SIMPLE LAWS THAT DESCRIBE HOW FORCES MAKE THINGS MOVE. THESE ARE CALLED **THE LAWS OF MOTION**.

NEWTON'S FIRST LAW OF MOTION

AN OBJECT AT REST WILL STAY AT REST UNLESS AN UNBALANCED FORCE ACTS UPON IT TO MOVE IT.

AN OBJECT IN MOTION WILL CONTINUE TO MOVE AT THE SAME SPEED AND IN THE SAME DIRECTION UNLESS A FORCE IS APPLIED TO CHANGE ITS DIRECTION OR STOP IT.
I WILL KEEP SLIDING UNTIL ACTED UPON BY A FORCE.
I SLIDE ACROSS THE ICE. I AM IN MOTION.
FRICTION BETWEEN THE ICE AND MY SHOES SLOWS MY MOTION AND EVENTUALLY BRING ME TO A STOP.
SEATBELTS AND AIRBAGS PLEASE!
NEWTON'S FIRST LAW PLAYS AN IMPORTANT ROLE IN ROAD SAFETY.
WHEN BRAKES ARE APPLIED SUDDENLY...
THE HEAD CONTINUES TO MOVE FORWARD.... UNTIL A FORCE IS APPLIED.
AN AIRBAG APPLIES FORCE ON THE HEAD AND STOPS ITS MOVEMENT GRADUALLY, PREVENTING INJURIES.
THE SEATBELT LOCKS STOP OUR BODY (WHICH IS IN MOVEMENT DUE TO INERTIA)

NEWTON'S SECOND LAW OF MOTION

WHEN A FORCE (PUSH OR PULL) IS APPLIED ON AN OBJECT, IT MOVES IN THE SAME DIRECTION AS THE FORCE.

IT ALSO DESCRIBES HOW MUCH AN OBJECT WILL ACCELERATE FOR A GIVEN NET FORCE.

LIGHTER OBJECTS CAN MOVE QUICKLY AND MORE EASILY WHEN ACTED UPON BY A FORCE.

SAME FORCE

HEAVIER THINGS REQUIRE MORE FORCE TO GET THEM MOVING.

IN OTHER WORDS, THE FORCE ACTING ON A BODY IS EQUAL TO THE PRODUCT OF ITS MASS AND ACCELERATION. IT CAN BE WRITTEN IN THE FORM, $F=ma$

NEWTON'S THIRD LAW OF MOTION

FOR EVERY ACTION, THERE IS AN EQUAL AND OPPOSITE REACTION.

ACCORDING TO ISAAC NEWTON, FORCES COME IN PAIRS. WHENEVER A FORCE ACTS IN ONE DIRECTION, IT CREATES AN EQUAL FORCE IN THE OPPOSITE DIRECTION.

THESE PAIRS ARE CALLED ACTION-REACTION PAIRS.

ACTION

THE WEIGHT OF PERSON PUSHES DOWN ON THE EARTH.

REACTION

THE GROUND PUSHES BACK TO THE PERSON WITH THE SAME FORCE.

OTHERWISE, THE PERSON WOULD SINK INTO THE GROUND!

ACTION-REACTION PAIRS ARE ALL AROUND US.

THE AIR PUSHES THE BALLOON IN THE OPPOSITE DIRECTION.

THE BALLOON PUSHES THE AIR OUT.

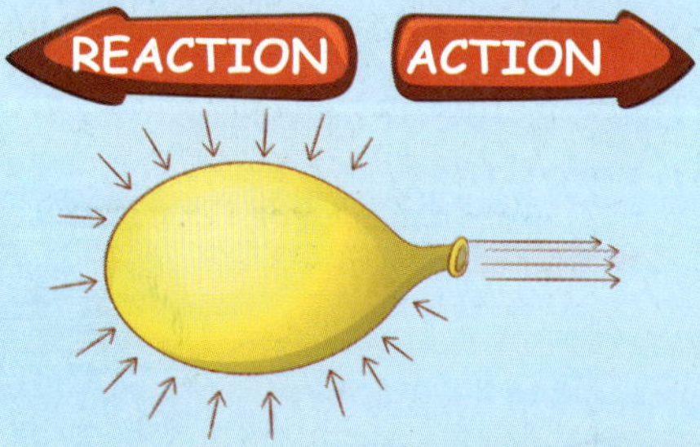

THE SKATER MOVES FORWARD IN THE OPPOSITE DIRECTION.

THE FOOT PUSHES ON THE GROUND.

APPLICATION OF NEWTON'S THIRD LAW CAN BE BEST SEEN IN A ROCKET.

THE ROCKET ENGINE PUSHES HOT GASES DOWNWARD

THE HOT GASES CREATE AN EQUAL OPPOSITE FORCE UPWARDS, WHICH PUSH AND SHOOT THE ROCKET UP INTO THE SKY.